At the Fun Fair

Level 4 – Blue

Helpful Hints for Reading at Home

The graphemes (written letters) and phonemes (units of sound) used throughout this series are aligned with Letters and Sounds. This offers a consistent approach to learning whether reading at home or in the classroom.

HERE IS A LIST OF PHONEMES FOR THIS PHASE OF LEARNING. AN EXAMPLE OF THE PRONUNCIATION CAN BE FOUND IN BRACKETS.

Phase 3			
j (jug)	v (van)	w (wet)	x (fox)
y (yellow)	z (zoo)	zz (buzz)	qu (quick)
ch (chip)	sh (shop)	th (thin/then)	ng (ring)
ai (rain)	ee (feet)	igh (night)	oa (boat)
oo (boot/look)	ar (farm)	or (for)	ur (hurt)
ow (cow)	oi (coin)	ear (dear)	air (fair)
ure (sure)	er (corner)		

HERE ARE SOME WORDS WHICH YOUR CHILD MAY FIND TRICKY.

Phase 3 Tricky Words			
he	you	she	they
we	all	me	are
be	my	was	her

Phase 4 Tricky Words			
said	were	have	there
like	little	so	one
do	when	some	out
come	what		

TOP TIPS FOR HELPING YOUR CHILD TO READ:

- Allow children time to break down unfamiliar words into units of sound and then encourage children to string these sounds together to create the word.

- Encourage your child to point out any focus phonics when they are used.

- Read through the book more than once to grow confidence.

- Ask simple questions about the text to assess understanding.

- Encourage children to use illustrations as prompts.

This book focuses on the phonemes /air/ and /ure/ and is a blue level 4 book band.

Can you sort all the words on this page into two groups?

Mature

Secure

Sure

Fair

Cured

Chair

Pairs

Pure

Hair

Airing

We are at the fun fair! There are a lot of fun things to do.

Shall we start on the cups? This will be fun, for sure. We can spin!

We might feel ill if we spin! Shall we go to the next thing?

It is a big fair!

Can you lure a duck with a stick?
Are you sure?

If you can lure a duck, you might win a gift!

Can you win one?

Look in the air. It is high up. Up and down we go!

There is a bar. It will keep us secure in the chair.

Bar

It has a big loop high in the air.
I can feel the wind in my hair!

Shall we get on? We must be mature if we go that high in the air.

Wow! What a good sight! I can see cars, roads and a farm.

Up the stairs and on to the cars next. Go left and right and...

... BUMP!

What is the best bit of the fair?

©2021 **BookLife Publishing Ltd.**
King's Lynn, Norfolk PE30 4LS

ISBN 978-1-83927-901-0

All rights reserved. Printed in England.
A catalogue record for this book is available from the British Library.

At the Fun Fair
Written by William Anthony
Designed by Drue Rintoul

An Introduction to BookLife Readers...

Our Readers have been specifically created in line with the London Institute of Education's approach to book banding and are phonetically decodable and ordered to support each phase of Letters and Sounds.

Each book has been created to provide the best possible reading and learning experience. Our aim is to share our love of books with children, providing both emerging readers and prolific page-turners with beautiful books that are guaranteed to provoke interest and learning, regardless of ability.

BOOK BAND GRADED using the Institute of Education's approach to levelling.

PHONETICALLY DECODABLE supporting each phase of Letters and Sounds.

EXERCISES AND QUESTIONS to offer reinforcement and to ascertain comprehension.

CLEAR DESIGN to inspire and provoke engagement, providing the reader with clear visual representations of each non-fiction topic.

AUTHOR INSIGHT:
WILLIAM ANTHONY

Despite his young age, William Anthony's involvement with children's education is quite extensive. He has written over 60 titles with BookLife Publishing so far, across a wide range of subjects. William graduated from Cardiff University with a 1st Class BA (Hons) in Journalism, Media and Culture, creating an app and a TV series, among other things, during his time there.

William Anthony has also produced work for the Prince's Trust, a charity created by HRH The Prince of Wales that helps young people with their professional future. He has created animated videos for a children's education company that works closely with the charity.

PHASE 3 AND 4 /air/ /ure/

This book focuses on the phonemes /air/ and /ure/ and is a blue level 4 book band.

Image Credits Images are courtesy of Shutterstock.com. With thanks to Getty Images, Thinkstock Photo and iStockphoto. Cover – Kristina Igumnova26, Pixel-Shot, ayelet-keshet. 4&5 – Visun Khankasem, passion3. 6&7 – Gregory E. Clifford, clearviewstock. 8&9 – ZikG, Nic Vilceanu. 10&11 – Nigel Jarvis, Martin Charles Hatch. 12&13 – snowturtle, Hung Chung Chih. 14&15 – Tomsickova Tatyana, MJTH.